THE BEST MEDICINE

"*Mind you, I will say this for euthanasia—no side effects.*"

THE BEST MEDICINE

Compiled and illustrated by

Graeme Garden

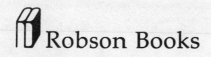

Robson Books

Author's royalties to Action Research for the Crippled Child

FIRST PUBLISHED IN GREAT BRITAIN IN 1984
BY ROBSON BOOKS LTD, BOLSOVER HOUSE,
5–6 CLIPSTONE STREET, LONDON W1P 7EB.
INTRODUCTORY MATERIAL © 1984 GRAEME
GARDEN. ILLUSTRATIONS COPYRIGHT © 1973,
1974, 1975 and 1976 *WORLD MEDICINE*

First impression September 1984
Second impression October 1984

British Library Cataloguing in Publication Data
Garden, Graeme
    The best medicine.
    1. Medicine—Anecdotes, facetiae, satire, etc.
    I. Title
    ISBN 0-86051-295-9

Typeset by Acorn Bookwork, Salisbury, Wilts.
Printed by Biddles Ltd, Guildford, Surrey

Contents

Acknowledgements Medicine would hardly be medicine without a sprinkling of personal specimens and samples, and this book is no exception. So it is with very great thanks that I acknowledge the invaluable help given by:

Eamonn Andrews
Ronnie Barker
Mr Jason Brice
Leslie Crowther
Paul Daniels
Robert Dougall
Paul Eddington
Dr Wendy Greengross and
    Mr Michael Humphrey
Lady Hamilton
Professor John Hermon-
    Taylor
James Herriot
Frankie Howerd
Gayle Hunnicutt
Miriam Karlin
Dr S. Mossman
Derek Nimmo
Maggie Philbin
Dr Oliver Pratt
Magnus Pyke
Robert Robinson
Professor R. Smithells

Dr Paul Standing
Dr William Tarnow-Mordi
Irene Thomas
Professor P. K. Thomas
Fred Trueman
Julie Walters
Kenneth Williams
Mike Yarwood

I would also like to thank Drs Dannie Abse, Miriam Stoppard, Edward Lowbury and Michael O'Donnell for permission to use extracts from their chapters in *My Medical School* (Robson Books, 1978), from which the late Lord Platt's reminiscences are also taken; and Dr Magnus Pyke for permission to use an extract from his book, *The Six Lives of Pyke* (J. M. Dent & Sons, 1981).

Finally, I am grateful to *World Medicine* for allowing me to reproduce the illustrations.

INTRODUCTION

This part of the book is called the Introduction. That is to say, having read or at least dipped into the rest of its pages, you have now turned to this bit to see what possible claims are being made for the book's right to exist. (Only publishers believe people read books by starting at the front.)

Well, this is a collection of funny medical stories. Some are old, some are new, some are borrowed, and some will appeal to those with a more clinical interest in bodily functions. Our many contributors come from both ends of the stethoscope, and while some of their stories are jokes, others are true—at least, they say they are true. I was surprised to receive accounts of one or two incidents, which friends of mine had told me were personal experiences, from another source entirely—the same stories, but featuring a different cast of characters. It's hard to believe that the story about the Coca-Cola bottle ever really happened—certainly not more than once—but in the other version I have heard, the bottle in question contained a well-known product which is dark, Irish and stout. And, on the subject of Eamonn Andrews, can we really believe that his doctor gives him regular check-ups by watching his TV performances? If so, is it a case of 'This Is Your Life In Their Hands'?

The examples of medical folklore you will find here should be given the benefit of the doubt. After all, there is an old saying in publishing circles: 'Truth is stranger than fiction—and it sells better.'

The aims of *The Best Medicine* are no more than the aims of every doctor and surgeon—to make you feel better, and to have you in stitches.

Graeme Garden B.A., M.B., B.Chir. (Cantab.)

A FINGER ON THE PULSE

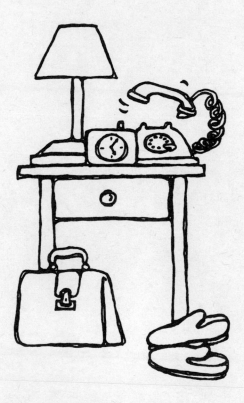

Doctors working in General Practice come in for their fair share of criticism. There was the case of the doctor, who called out a plumber to deal with a blocked lavatory at three o'clock in the morning. The bleary-eyed plumber turned up, dropped two aspirins into the loo, said 'If it's no better tomorrow, give me a call', and went home.

On the other hand, General Practice often brings out the best in the profession. A dedicated Lancashire GP I know was called out one night by a farmer whose small son was 'burning up with the fever'. The doctor was told how to find the right road over the Fells, then to turn into a gateway, and a mile or so up the lane he would come to the remote farmhouse. To help him find it, the farmer said he would hang a lantern on the gate.

After three hours of searching along treacherous roads in driving snow, the GP had seen no sign of a lantern glowing in the dark. Eventually he gave up and went home, where he phoned the farmer.

'Oh,' said the farmer, 'about an hour after I called, Johnny got much better and we decided not to bother you, so I took the lantern down.'

DOCTOR: Would you like me to give you a local anaesthetic?

PATIENT: No, BUPA's paying for this—give me something imported.

Answering his telephone at three o'clock one morning, a doctor heard one of his patients asking, 'Doctor, can you come over immediately? I've got terrible toothache.'

'Madam,' replied the doctor, trying to restrain himself, 'with the greatest respect, you need a dentist, not a doctor.'

'I know I do,' said the voice at the other end of the line, 'but I didn't have the heart to disturb a dentist at this hour of the night.'

DOCTOR: What's Mr MacDougall complaining about now?

NURSE: He says he recovered before all the medicine was used up and he wants a refund on the prescription.

As an elderly patient neared his end, his doctor called his relatives to his bedside to pay their final respects; but as is often the case they started telling him how much better he was looking. 'Your colour's better,' said someone brightly. 'The doctor says your heart sounds stronger', added another. 'And you seem to be breathing more easily,' a third told him.

'That's good,' replied the patient. 'It's reassuring to know that I'm going to die cured.'

Following the death of one of his private patients, a doctor presented his bill to the executor of the will and asked whether he wished to have it sworn to.

14

'That will not be necessary,' he was told. 'My late client's death is sufficient evidence that you attended him professionally.'

'Doctor, doctor, I feel like a bell.'
'Take two of these pills, and if they don't work, give me a ring.'

An irate mother took her young son to the surgery and asked the doctor whether a boy of twelve could remove his own appendix.

'No, of course not,' laughed the doctor.

'There,' said the mother, cuffing her son round the head, 'what did I tell you! Now you just put it back!'

DOCTOR: You look exhausted.
PATIENT: I am. After your nurse telephoned yesterday and said you wanted to do a blood test, I sat up all night mugging it up.

"Now come on doctor, you've had enough clues—just one more guess . . ."

Overheard in a pub:
'The doctor said he would have me on my feet in a fortnight.'
'And did he?'
'Yes, I had to sell my car to pay the bill.'

DOCTOR: There goes the only woman I ever loved.
NURSE: Why don't you marry her?
DOCTOR: I can't afford to. She's my best patient.

'All this for only a few hours' work?' an American doctor asked when he collected his car from a garage after a service. 'That's almost as much as I'd charge if you'd been to see me.'

'Why, I reckon that's how it should be,' replied the garage owner. 'You doctors have been working on the same model for getting on for two thousand years, but we get new models coming in here all the time.'

Sign in a chemist's during alterations:
BISMUTH AS USUAL. OPIUM 9.00 A.M. TO 7.00 P.M.

A doctor called on the wife of a recently-deceased patient to tell her that in view of her bereavement he was going to halve his fee.

'That is kind of you,' the lady replied, 'and in view of your generosity, I will forego the other half.'

'I just feel that everybody is taking advantage of me, doctor,' confessed one patient.

'That's absolute rubbish,' replied the doctor, 'just go home and forget all about it.'

'Thank you so much, I feel better already,' said the patient. 'How much do I owe you?'

'How much can you afford?'

16

DOCTOR: How's your husband's lumbago?
WIFE: Not so good, doctor. I rubbed his back with whisky, like you told me, but he ricked his neck trying to lick it off.

A notorious hypochondriac who had established himself as the life and soul of most dinner-parties with outlandish descriptions of his various ailments, sat through one evening scarcely saying a word.

'What's the matter?' asked his hostess. 'Don't tell me it's so awful you can't even talk about it.'

'It's not that,' replied the guest. 'It's just that I went to a new doctor this morning and he cured all my topics of conversation.'

'I don't know what I'm going to do,' complained one young man to a friend in the pub. 'My girlfriend has started going round with that new doctor who's just moved in.'

'Try giving her an apple a day,' suggested the other.

'Have you tried these new slimming pills?' a woman asked her friend who was also trying to shed a few pounds.

'No, I haven't. Mind you, with the diet I'm on at the moment, I've enough on my plate as it is.'

A cold is both positive and negative; sometimes the eyes have it, sometimes the nose.

DOCTOR: Tell your wife that her deafness is really nothing to worry about, it's simply a sign of advancing years.
HUSBAND: Er ... would you mind telling her that yourself, doctor?

"You misheard, Mr Hargreaves—I did not recommend a course of grope therapy!"

A patient suffering from insomnia was told by her doctor to be sure that she never went to bed on an empty stomach, but always had something to eat first.

'But, once you told me never to eat before going to bed,' replied the puzzled patient.

'That was last year,' her doctor reassured her, 'medicine has made enormous advances since then.'

PATIENT: Doctor, I got a pound coin stuck in my ear a fortnight ago.
DOCTOR: Why didn't you come to see me about it then?
PATIENT: I didn't need the money until now.

A doctor was examining a boy in his surgery. Suddenly he nipped out and asked his receptionist for a screwdriver. A moment or two later he was out again, this time asking for a hammer and cold chisel. When he came out a third time, the boy's mother asked anxiously, 'For goodness' sake, doctor, what's the matter with him?'

'I don't know. I haven't had a chance to examine him yet . . . I'm still trying to get my bag open.'

PATIENT: Doctor, I've got this rash right across my chest.
DOCTOR: Have you had this rash before?
PATIENT: Yes, I have.
DOCTOR: Well, you've got it again.

An anxious mother, explaining why she had brought her son to surgery, told her GP: 'It's his head, doctor. He's had it on and off ever since he was born.'

A young man arrived one morning at the surgery of an eminent bone specialist and told the receptionist that he wished to see the doctor privately.

'Have you an appointment?'

'No.'

'Then this is your first visit here?'

"You promised not to laugh!"

'Yes.'

'Right, go into the dressing-room and take off all your clothes. When the bell rings, go through the door marked "Consulting Room".'

The man tried to protest, but the nurse was adamant that no exceptions could be made to the doctor's orders and eventually he did as he was told. The bell rang a couple of minutes after he had undressed and he went in to see the great man.

'What's wrong with you?' bellowed the specialist. 'You look healthy enough to me.'

'Nothing.'

'Nothing? Well, what the hell are you doing here?'

'I just called to see if you wanted to renew your subscription to *The Lancet*.'

DOCTOR: What do you do for a living?
PATIENT: I'm a magician.
DOCTOR: That's unusual. What's your best trick?
PATIENT: I saw a woman in half.
DOCTOR: And is that very difficult?
PATIENT: No, it's child's play. I learned how to do it when I was a kid.
DOCTOR: Have you got any brothers or sisters?
PATIENT: I had two half-sisters . . .

PATIENT: Doctor, if this swelling in my leg gets any worse I won't be able to get my trousers on.
DOCTOR: Don't worry, I'll give you a prescription.
PATIENT: What's it for?
DOCTOR: A kilt.

An unfortunate doctor lived next door to a hypochondriac who thought nothing of knocking him up at any hour asking for something for a headache or a tummy upset.

The doctor tolerated this for several years until, much to his relief, the man died. Sadly the doctor, too, passed

"It's what we doctors call 'aversion therapy' ..."

away a couple of years later and was buried next to his former neighbour. On his first night in the cemetery there was a loud knocking on the side of his coffin and a familiar voice said, 'Sorry to bother you, doctor, but can you give me something for worms ... ?'

DOCTOR: How may fingers am I holding up?
PATIENT: Six.
DOCTOR: I don't know if your eyesight is bad, or just your arithmetic.

There's a new book on the market called The Hypochondriac's Almanac. *It's the ideal gift for the person who has everything.*

"To be honest, Mrs Cosgrove, I've always thought of you as just another problem patient—that is until these gentlemen showed an interest in your case . . ."

In an effort to reassure one of his patients that there was nothing seriously wrong with him, the doctor told him to spend more time in the fresh air, walking at least a mile or two each day. 'And what's your line of business?' he asked.

'I'm a long-distance runner,' replied the man.

'What has happened to you?' a GP asked a patient who came to see him with two badly burned ears.

'My wife was doing the ironing while we were watching the telly. She had the iron near the phone and when it rang I answered the iron.'

'But what happened to the other ear?'

'Just as I hung up, the phone rang again.'

DOCTOR: Have you finished that medicine I gave you?
PATIENT: I haven't even started it yet, doctor. The label says that I must keep the top screwed on tightly the whole time.

A heavy smoker who was concerned about the advertising encouraging him to give up, asked his doctor: 'Is it really true that smoking will shorten my days?'

'Certainly,' exclaimed the doctor. 'I gave up once and the days seem about a hundred hours long.'

A recently-qualified GP prescribed some suppositories for one of his less erudite patients, telling him to insert one in his rectum each morning and evening and to come back a week later. At the next consultation it was obvious that the man hadn't followed the doctor's instructions. 'Have you been doing what I told you?' asked the doctor.

' 'Course I have.'

'Inserting them in your rectum?'

'Yes . . . what do you expect me to do, stick them up my ruddy arse?'

'Doctor, doctor, I feel like a sheet of music.'
'Really? I must take some notes.'

"It's the girl at the answering service—she's got this funny pain . . ."

A GP in a country practice came round a bend in his car one wet evening, hit a patch of mud, skidded and rolled over into the ditch. Dazed, but otherwise unharmed, he stumbled to a nearby house to ring the local garage. The lady of the house was just putting down the phone when he knocked at the door. 'Oh doctor, I've only just rung your wife, how clever of you to get here so quickly. There's been the most awful accident outside.'

DOCTOR: My treatment is obviously doing you good. You're looking much better.
PATIENT: Oh, thank you. I always look better in this hat.

A husband at home with flu was visited by his doctor, who took the liberty of kissing the man's wife as he left

"Yes—yes—of course I'll sign the sick note, Mr Hooley. . ."

the house. Unknown to the doctor, the patient had witnessed this, and under great provocation almost hit him with a milk bottle. However, he managed to restrain himself out of respect for the doctor's profession—and thumped his wife instead.

DOCTOR: Did you wash your neck before coming to see me?
BOY: Of course I did.
DOCTOR (*taking cotton wool, dipping it in surgical spirit, and wiping it across the boy's neck*): What about this dirt then?
BOY: That doesn't count . . . that's dry cleaning.

PATIENT: It is good of you to visit me, doctor, but isn't it a little out of your way?
DOCTOR: No, not really. I've got another patient near here, so I thought I might as well kill two birds with one stone.

An Indian opened the door to a doctor's waiting-room and walked straight through to the door of the surgery on the other side, ignoring the other patients dutifully waiting to be called in. As he was about to open the door, a woman jumped up, caught him by the arm and said in a loud, distinct voice: 'No. We before you. You take your turn. Understand?'

The Indian answered in the same careful tones: 'No. You after me. Me doctor. Understand?'

'Doctor, doctor, I feel like an old sock.'
  'Well, I'll be darned!'

DOCTOR: I suppose you went to another doctor before you came to see me?

PATIENT: No, I went to the chemist.
DOCTOR: And what idiotic advice did he give you?
PATIENT: He told me to come to you.

A middle-aged couple arrived at their GP's surgery, the wife helping her husband through the door and into a chair. When they were called, the man got to his feet in obvious pain and, bent at the waist, shuffled into the doctor's consulting room.

'Arthritis with complications?' asked the receptionist sympathetically.

'Do-it-yourself,' replied the wife tartly, 'with concrete paving slabs.'

DOCTOR: I think it would be a good idea to stop taking those sleeping pills before they become a habit.
PATIENT: Don't be silly. I've been taking these for fifteen years, and they haven't become a habit yet.

"Now that's what I call a case of dandruff."

When a phone call came through to say that a child had got a biro stuck in his ear, the doctor told the mother that he would be over right away. 'Stay calm,' he said, 'and tell me what you're going to do until I get there.'

'I suppose I'll have to make do with a pencil,' she said, 'but try not to be too long.'

PATIENT: Tell me honestly, doctor, what's the matter with me?
DOCTOR: You eat too much, drink too much, and you're the laziest man I've ever treated.
PATIENT: Terrific, but do you think you could pop that into Latin, so that I can take a week off work?

Definition of an alcoholic: A person who drinks more than his own doctor.

At the end of a consultation a doctor told his lady patient: 'Now, remember what I've told you. You need to take regular baths, have plenty of fresh air and wear warm clothes.'

That evening her husband asked how she had got on at the surgery. 'He said I've got to be very careful with myself,' she began. 'I need a holiday in the Mediterranean, then a trip to the Alps, and he says I must have a new winter coat immediately.'

DOCTOR: Mrs Hartnoll, I've got news for you.
PATIENT: Excuse me, it's *Miss* Hartnoll.
DOCTOR: In that case, Miss Hartnoll, I've got bad news for you.

A spinster who prided herself on her independence broke her leg riding, and was forced to stay in plaster for several weeks while the fracture healed. During that time she constantly pestered her doctor to have the cast removed, and when the time eventually came for it to come off she asked him, 'Is it all right for me to climb the stairs now?'

'By all means,' replied the doctor.

'I'm so glad,' she said. 'I'm fed up with shinning up the drainpipe all the time.'

"Well, I'd say the loss of appetite was just another of those annoying little side-effects, Mr Cosgrove."

'Did your husband die a natural death?' a recently-bereaved woman was asked.

'Oh, no,' she said. 'We had the doctor in to see him.'

Barely half-an-hour after he'd climbed into bed having attended a night call, the doctor's phone rang and a young man screamed down the line: 'You'd better come quickly. My wife's got a terrible pain in her stomach and I'm sure it's her appendix.'

'Don't be silly,' said the doctor. 'It'll be indigestion. Just give her a glass of Andrews and tell her to come and see me in the morning if it still hurts.' But the husband insisted that doctor came immediately and kept repeating that it was her appendix. 'Well it can't be,' shouted the doctor losing his temper. 'Her appendix was taken out a couple of years ago. Have you ever heard of anyone having two appendices?'

'Have you ever heard of anyone having two wives?' replied the husband.

DOCTOR: Did those pills I gave you help you sleep any better?
PATIENT: Well, I slept—but I still dreamed that I didn't.

SPECIALIST TREATMENT

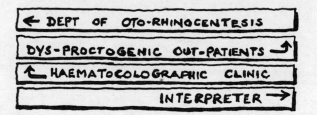

← DEPT OF OTO-RHINOCENTESIS

DYS-PROCTOGENIC OUT-PATIENTS ↱

↰ HAEMATOCOLOGRAPHIC CLINIC

INTERPRETER →

What is so special about Specialists? Specialists suffer from two problems. First, their patients think the Specialist knows everything. Second, so does the Specialist.

A pal of mine, whose particular interest is gastro-intestinal surgery, was once taking a well-earned weekend break at a small country hotel. There he was collared by a man who, discovering my friend's line of work, spent the entire evening treating him to an account of his bowel problems, asking his opinion of the condition, the treatment he'd been getting, and demanding advice. Of course, it ruined the surgeon's enjoyment of his holiday, and that night he phoned his brother, who is a solicitor.

'Can I', he asked, 'charge this pest a fee for consultation?'

His brother agreed that he could—after all the man had approached him for a professional opinion.

The surgeon was delighted—until he returned home and found his brother's bill waiting for him.

Faced with an ever-increasing problem of drug abuse, French doctors tried a novel remedy and jubilantly announced that they had found a cure for addicts after thirteen of the twenty trial patients had successfully completed the therapy. They had all been sent on ocean cruises.

"His technique's a bit unorthodox, but always entertaining."

PATIENT: I'm terrified. This is the first operation I've ever had.

SURGEON: I know just how you feel; this is the first operation I've ever done.

A patient was trying to persuade his doctor that an operation wasn't really necessary. 'Honestly, doctor,' he said, 'the gallstones aren't a problem. They just itch a little.'

'We'll still need to open you up,' he was told.

'But why?'

'Otherwise, how are we going to scratch them?'

DOCTOR: It'll cost £600 for this operation.
PATIENT: Isn't it possible to have it done for nearer £300?
DOCTOR: It might be . . . but the surgeon will have to use blunt instruments.

'What kind of job do you do?' a lady passenger asked the man travelling in her compartment.

'I'm a naval surgeon,' he replied.

'Goodness!' said the lady. 'How you doctors specialize these days!'

Surgeon to colleague: 'We operated just in time. A couple more days and he would have recovered without us.'

An eminent surgeon went to spend Easter with his identical twin who had recently been installed as the vicar in a country parish. Walking round the village one morning, he met one of his brother's parishioners who congratulated him on his sermon on Easter Day.

'I am afraid you are mistaken,' replied the surgeon. 'I am not the brother that preaches; I am the one who practises.'

PATIENT: Can this operation be performed successfully, doctor?
DOCTOR: That's what we're about to find out . . .

A little girl went to the dentist to have a tooth removed for the first time. She seemed more than usually nervous, and to settle her for the extraction the dentist gave her a tranquillizer.

'Feeling braver now?' he asked when this had taken effect.

'You bet!' she said. 'I'd like to see anybody try and yank out my tooth now.'

A patient grumbling about dental charges told his dentist: 'Five pounds seems an awful lot for pulling out a tooth in less than thirty seconds.'

'I could always pull it slowly, if you prefer,' replied the dentist.

James Whistler, the Victorian artist, showed scant respect for the hierarchy of any profession, and when his poodle fell ill with a throat infection he sent immediately for the country's leading ENT specialist, Sir Morell Mackenzie. The great man was not amused when he was shown his patient, but he conducted a thorough examination, wrote out a prescription, and left with his fee.

The next day Whistler received a message from Mackenzie asking him to call on him without delay. Fearing some development in the poodle's condition, Whistler hurried to the doctor's house.

'So good of you to come, Mr Whistler,' said Mackenzie as his visitor was shown in. 'I wanted to see you about having my front door painted.'

What did the woman say when she climbed out of the plastic surgeon's chair?
'Thanks for the lift.'

PATIENT: Will my appendix scar show, doctor?
SURGEON: Not if you're careful.

"I know you won't mind the intrusion, but they tell me you're a medical man . . ."

Sir Frederick Treves, he of *The Elephant Man* fame, once told a patient complaining about the discomfort of his condition: 'My dear sir, allow me to congratulate you. You are the lucky possessor of an illness which hitherto has been thought to be extinct.'

SAILOR: I'm getting married, sir, but before I do, there's something I must get off my chest.
MEDICAL OFFICER: What's that?
SAILOR: A tattoo with 'I love Alice' on it.

A successful skin specialist was asked late in life why he had followed that particular aspect of medicine, and replied: 'The answer is very simple. My patients never get me out of bed at night; they never die of the complaint; and they never recover.'

PATIENT: I'm afraid I've broken my glasses ... will I have to be examined all over again?
OPTICIAN: No, just your eyes.

'This is Dr Morrison,' said a hostess, introducing her distinguished guest to a lady friend, who professed to know everything about everyone.

'Doctor, I'm so pleased to meet you,' began the woman. 'I know I shouldn't really be asking you this, but my husband's been getting this regular pain in his head and I was wondering ...'

'Excuse me, madam,' he cut in, 'but I'm a Doctor of Economics.'

'Quite so,' replied the lady, '... and I was just wondering whether he should lighten his holding in ICI?'

PATIENT: Are you fond of shellfish, doctor?
DOCTOR: I wouldn't say I was fond of them, but I'm very grateful to them.

Graffito in an osteopath's:
For you I'll work my fingers to the bone.

A woman went to see a stomach specialist, who spent a long time rubbing and manipulating her stomach. 'How was that?' he asked when he'd finished.

'That was great, doctor,' she said, 'but I really came to see you about this pain in my right knee ...'

Still flushed with examination success, a recently-qualified doctor spent a weekend with his proud parents and took the opportunity to call on the family doctor, whom he now regarded as a colleague.

'I suppose you're going to specialize,' remarked the elder.

'Oh, yes,' said the young doctor, 'in the diseases of the nose. In my opinion, the diseases of the ears and throat are too complicated to be combined satisfactorily with the nose for the purposes of modern study and treatment.'

'Is that so?' said the family doctor. 'And on which nostril do you propose to concentrate?'

NURSE: Who is your family doctor?
PATIENT: It's hard to say.
NURSE: Surely you must know the name?
PATIENT: It's not as easy as that—it's just that mother goes to an eye doctor, father to a stomach specialist, my brother is being treated by a psychiatrist, and I'm under the osteopath.

"I sometimes think he takes his heroic surgery too far."

'My patient is such a hypochondriac,' said one doctor, 'that he reads the obituary columns just to cheer himself up.'

'That's nothing,' replied his colleague. 'I've got one who reads them as soon as he wakes up every morning just to check that he's still alive.'

An elderly man undergoing a course of rejuvenation therapy was starting to get restless. 'Keep still,' his doctor told him, 'how am I expected to work with you wriggling around like this.'

A few moments later the man started sobbing. 'Don't worry,' the doctor told him, 'the pain will soon go.'

'It's not that I'm crying about,' said his patient. 'I'm worried I'm going to be late for school.'

PATIENT: I'd rather have a baby than have a tooth out.
DENTIST: Well, make up your mind—I'll have to alter the position of the chair.

Advertisement in a local newspaper:
Owing to illness, dentist requires man/woman until September as stop-gap receptionist.

DOCTOR: If it comes to an operation, do you think you'll be able to pay?
PATIENT: Put it this way, doctor, if I can't pay, will it still come to an operation?

A man went to have his eyes tested. The optician told him to put his left hand over his right eye and to read the chart, but he didn't seem to know his left from his right.

'OK,' said the optician, 'just put your right hand over your right eye,' but that didn't improve matters. So the optician cut a hole in a piece of card and held it in front of the patient's face, so that only his right eye was exposed; but as soon as he did this, the patient began complaining.

'Now what's the matter?' asked the optician.

'I wanted a pair of metal frames like my brother . . .'

One of the unfortunate consequences of having a duodenal ulcer afflicted a vicar, who found that whenever he blew out the candles in his church, his breath burst into flames. This disagreeable condition was caused by the build-up of inflammable gas brought about by the ulcer. In the words of a hospital spokesman after an operation, the vicar 'was able to carry out his duties in a more decorous fashion'.

"A major breakthrough gentlemen—the cardio-pulmonary cerebro-visceral bypass unit! It replaces the entire patient."

YOUNG SURGEON: I operated on that old fellow yesterday for appendicitis.

OLD SURGEON: Really? What was the matter with him?

OPTICIAN: There's nothing wrong with your daughter's eyes.

MOTHER: What's the matter with her, then?

OPTICIAN: I think her pigtails are too tight.

What's the simplest cure for double vision?
    Shut one eye.

In the middle of an appalling Highland winter, word reached the outside world that a small community way up in the Cairngorms had been cut off for weeks and were running perilously low on food and medical supplies. In spite of the howling blizzards and arctic temperatures, a rescue team was air-lifted to them and managed to force its way up the glen and into the tiny village. Knocking at the door of the first house, the leader of the party called out: 'We're from the Red Cross.'

'You've no' come at a good time,' shouted back a voice from inside. 'We've had a cruel winter here and there's no' a penny to spare to give you.'

YOUNG DOCTOR: Do you mind if I ask why you always ask your patients what they have eaten?

OLD DOCTOR: Not at all, my boy. Their food is very important; it helps me gauge my fees.

Graffito on the notice-board of a laboratory:
    A researcher learns more and more about less and less until he knows everything about nothing.

YOUNG DOCTOR: How did you become a doctor?
OLD DOCTOR: I started as a patient and worked my way up.

A specialist is one who has his patients trained to be ill only during surgery hours, whereas a general practitioner can be called off the golf course at any time.

SHRINK TO ME ONLY

Would you care to lie down on the couch?

I have seen psychiatrists defined as doctors who go down deeper, stay down longer, and come up filthier. This is not absolutely true in all cases.

Two fellow medical students of mine turned into psychiatrists. Both now practise in America, where they tell me that psychiatry is much the same as in Britain, except that the pay is better and the patients tend to carry guns.

Doctors, of course, are as likely to go crazy as anyone else. On one occasion a GP we can call Smith had a problem which became so severe that his friend Dr Brown had to drive him to be admitted to a psychiatric hospital many miles from his practice.

On their arrival they were greeted by the matron, who said, 'Ah, you've come to deliver Dr Smith.'

'That's right,' said Dr Smith, 'this is Dr Smith,' and handed over the bewildered Dr Brown.

'No, no, I'm Dr Brown,' protested Brown.

'Of course you are,' said the matron, as two burly orderlies took him away to be locked up.

Meanwhile the gleeful Dr Smith pinched the car and drove off into the night.

NURSE:	Are you still treating the patient who thought he was a tailor?
PSYCHIATRIST:	Yes, I am.
NURSE:	When are you going to cure him?
PSYCHIATRIST:	Just as soon as he's finished making my suit.

After what was glowingly described as 'a brilliant interview' a new medical superintendent was appointed to the principal prison in the state of Indiana—a post that commanded 35,000 dollars a year. However, his tenure was somewhat short-lived. Local newspapers featuring the appointment also printed a photograph of the successful candidate. He was immediately recognized by the staff of the state's largest lunatic asylum. The new medical superintendent turned out to be an inmate who had absconded in a disused icebox a couple of days before his prison appointment.

Definition of psychiatry: The care of the id by the odd.

A woman who had been undergoing psychiatric treatment for some time asked her psychiatrist if it would be all right for her to go to Venice for a short holiday, and was given his blessing.

A short time later he received a postcard from her saying: 'Having a wonderful time. Why?'

DOCTOR:	What seems to be the problem?
PATIENT:	I can't stop eating dates.
DOCTOR:	What's wrong with that?
PATIENT:	I've run out of calendars.

A new patient arrived at a psychiatrist's consulting room, was shown to the couch by the psychiatrist and asked to relax fully, before the consultation began.

'Since this is your first visit to me,' the psychiatrist began, 'and I know absolutely nothing about you, why don't you tell me about yourself from the beginning?'

'Fine,' said the patient. 'In the beginning I created Heaven and Earth . . .'

A psychiatrist received a frantic telephone call from a kleptomaniac at three o'clock in the morning. 'I'm sorry to ring at this time, doctor, but I feel dreadful. I've got a terrible urge to steal again.'

'For heaven's sake,' replied the doctor, 'just take a couple of ashtrays and call me again in the morning.'

PATIENT:	Doctor, I keep thinking I'm a dog.
PSYCHIATRIST:	How long have you felt like this?
PATIENT:	Ever since I was a puppy.
PSYCHIATRIST:	Just lie down on the couch.
PATIENT:	I'm not allowed on the furniture.

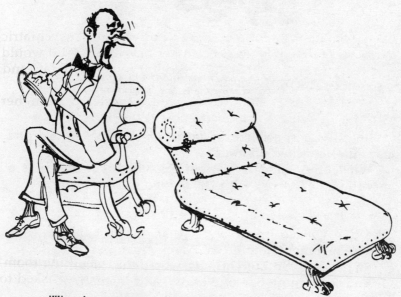

What do you mean—all psychiatrists are nutters?

What is the difference between a psychopath and a neurotic?
  A psychopath knows for certain that two times two is five.
A neurotic knows that two times two is four, but it bothers
him.

"I only came to a psychiatrist in the first place because
I needed someone to feel superior to."

'Why do you specialize in treating schizophrenics?' one
psychiatrist asked another.
  'What other kind of patient can you send two bills a
month and get away with it?' replied his colleague.

'We like you so much better than the last doctor,' one
inmate of a mental home told a new member of staff.
  'That's very kind of you,' answered the doctor. 'Why?'
  'You seem more like one of us,' said the patient.

PSYCHIATRIST:	Now, relaxation is terribly important in your case. What do you do to unwind?
PATIENT:	I shoot flies with a bow and arrow.
PSYCHIATRIST:	Isn't that terribly messy?
PATIENT:	Oh no, I only aim at their legs.

Mrs Nancy Gordon paid a visit to a mental hospital in Des Moines, Iowa in 1950, to visit her elderly aunt. Sadly she arrived to the news that the old lady had passed away, but as a consolation the sister offered to show her her room. While looking round it Mrs Gordon felt a bit drowsy and lay down on the bed for forty winks. The next thing she knew, she was being woken by a doctor telling her he was moving her to another room. She did as she was told and ended up staying in the hospital for the next twenty-five years, until the mistake had been discovered. When asked about her experience, she said philosophically that she was the sort of person who believed in letting life follow its natural course.

A man arrived at a psychiatrist's consulting room in a very distressed state. 'I keep getting these awful nightmares,' he explained. 'Every night it's the same. I find myself in a large room with dozens of gorgeous girls.'

'What's so awful about that?' asked the psychiatrist.

'In the dream, I'm a girl too!'

'Is she being treated because she is highly strung?'

'Goodness, no. With her income she's rich enough to be psychoneurotic.'

| PSYCHIATRIST: | Now that you're finally cured of your delusion, why are you looking so sad? |
| PATIENT: | Wouldn't you be sad if yesterday you were God and today you're nobody? |

51

A man went to see a psychiatrist about his sister. 'She keeps breaking thermometers,' he told him, 'drinks the mercury and throws the glass away.'

'What!' screamed the psychiatrist. 'That's the best bit!'

A Gloucestershire man who was taken to court for a number of driving offences told local magistrates: 'My mind was preoccupied with the thought of my grandson, who is in hospital with a broken thigh; my mother, who is seriously ill in another hospital; my wife, who is caring for my 80 year-old mother-in-law; and my sister who has collapsed under the strain of looking after her—to say nothing of the stress involved in the reorganizing of local government.'

MASOCHIST: Beat me, beat me!
SADIST: No!

'Doctor, doctor, I must talk to you about my husband. He thinks he's an olive.'

'Why do you say that?'

'He keeps sticking his head in other people's martinis.'

'Your husband is suffering from complete mental exhaustion,' a doctor told a woman who had brought the patient to the surgery. 'He's in a very serious condition. You really should have brought him to see me much earlier.'

'But I couldn't,' she replied. 'When he was in his right mind he absolutely refused to have a doctor.'

PSYCHIATRIST: Perhaps you'd like to tell me about this dream that's been worrying you.
PATIENT: Well, I dreamed I was walking down the street with nothing on except for a hat.

PSYCHIATRIST: And were you embarrassed?
PATIENT: I certainly was, It was last year's hat.'

"Darling, we can't go on meeting like this . . ."

'Now then,' said the psychiatrist to two schizophrenics, 'why don't the five of us sit down and talk this thing out?'

"I see what you mean about the loss of libido, Mrs Fenton . . ."

Years ago a Hungarian bee-keeper was travelling by train to Budapest with some of his bees. For safety's sake the insects were being carried in milk bottles sealed with brown paper. However, in the course of their long journey, some of the bees got a bit fractious and made a bid to escape. Several of them succeeded in penetrating the paper and crawled up their owner's trouser legs. To avoid the painful consequences, he politely asked the other passengers if they would mind leaving the compartment while he removed his trousers. This they agreed to do. The bee-keeper gingerly slipped them off his legs, but just as he thought he was safe, a passing express set up such a draught, that the trousers were blown into the corridor, where they wrapped themselves round the head of the ticket collector, against whom the bees then turned their vengeance. One of the other passengers pulled the communication cord, the train screeched to a halt—and then burst into flames. With the situation fast getting out of control, the bee-keeper decided to make a run for it, but was quickly apprehended and taken to the nearest asylum. There he spent three days retelling his story until the doctors were finally convinced that he was sane.

PATIENT: Doctor, I'm scared to death of birds. Even a tiny sparrow brings me out in a cold sweat.
PSYCHIATRIST: But why are you afraid of birds?
PATIENT: Aren't most worms?

HOSPITAL ROUNDS

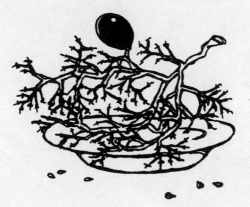

I was there when the Consultant asked the old man, 'Well, what's brought you into hospital?' and got the reply, 'An ambulance, doctor.'

What goes on in hospitals is often mystifying to the patients; it's also as mystifying to the doctors.

Many years ago the great orthopaedic surgeon and pioneer, T. P. MacMurray, was conducting a ward round with his students. One would-be surgeon was asked to comment on a particularly complicated case, and launched into a long and involved account of his opinions. MacMurray stopped him. 'Come with me,' he said.

He led his team to the entrance hall of the hospital. There he stopped in front of a beautiful Victorian painting that hung on the wall, showing a dedicated doctor at the bedside of a dying girl, her parents in the background looking on while her life ebbed away as dawn broke outside the window.

'You,' said MacMurray to the student, 'are just like that doctor in the painting.'

'Am I, sir?'

'Yes. You don't bloody know.'

When a schoolboy got his head stuck in a vase, his mother took the sensible precaution of whisking him off to Casualty without trying to free him herself. However, in order to attract as little attention as possible, she put his school cap on top of the vase as they travelled by bus to the hospital.

PATIENT: That other doctor doesn't seem to share your diagnosis.

DOCTOR: I know, but your post mortem will prove that I am right.

"Nice one, Mr Copdock."

During his time at Oxford, Sir William Osler visited one of the leading hospitals in London and was given a conducted tour by the senior medical staff. He examined a number of charts at the foot of the patients' beds and noted the familiar abbreviations for their particular conditions: TB for Tuberculosis, SF for Scarlet Fever, D for Diptheria, and so on. Most of the illnesses seemed to be well in hand, the only notable exception being the one indicated by the initials GOK.

Remarking on the epidemic of GOK which seemed to have laid low a significant number of patients, Sir William asked what the abbreviation stood for, since he had never encountered it in his native North America.

'It's for when diagnosis is a little uncertain, sir,' came the reply. 'God Only Knows.'

In spite of several warnings that they were conversing with a machine, over half the patients who consulted a medical computer in a Connecticut hospital insisted that they must have been talking to a human being. As one of them remarked: 'No machine could understand me that well.'

Graffito in medical school:
All gall is divided into three parts: bladder, stones and unmitigated.

DOCTOR: How is the little boy who swallowed a fifty-pence coin?
NURSE: No change yet, doctor.

A father-to-be who made enquiries about reserving his wife a bed in a maternity home, received the disappointing reply that beds were at a premium at the time in question, and that if he wanted one reserved, he should have applied ten months in advance.

WIFE: Did you say that my husband was shot in the woods?
DOCTOR: No, I said he'd been hit in the lumbar region.

61

"Course I didn't like to disturb my own doctor just for this . . ."

A patient operated on in a Teesside hospital was found to contain the following items in his stomach: fragments of metal and china, matches, a key, a knife, a razor-blade, a hair-grip, a football coupon, a pin, nails, a selection of stones, pre-decimal coinage to the value of 4½d, a pen-nib, a pair of dividers and a double-six domino.

Appealing against her sacking from a Birmingham hospital, a nurse explained that, far from spitting in front of her matron, she had been removing her chewing gum before speaking to a superior.

62

A man carried into a hospital casualty department face down on a stretcher, explained in embarrassed tones that he had a Coca Cola bottle stuck fast that prevented him from sitting down. The doctor attending him was at a loss as to how to extract it without breaking it and causing further injury; until an idea came to him. He bent a piece of stiff wire into a corkscrew, pushed this through the open end of the bottle, which was still accessible, and filled it with plaster of Paris. When this had set, he was able gently to remove it. The patient was full of gratitude, though a little non-plussed by the student nurse who asked innocently: 'However did you swallow it in the first place?'

DOCTOR: How's the woman who swallowed a spoon?
NURSE: She hasn't stirred at all.

"Just drop your trousers, Mr Colton, then we'll see what's what."

After the loss of his sight for four years, Dan Hoke, from Ashland, Kentucky, underwent a successful eye operation. His wife was waiting by his bedside as the bandages were removed. Looking up at her with wonder, Dan said, 'Boy, you sure have gotten fat in four years.'

PATIENT: Doctor! Please close the curtains, or the man across the street will see me naked.

DOCTOR: I shouldn't worry. If he catches sight of you like that, he'll probably close the curtains himself.

'How's your husband today?' one neighbour asked another.

'Much worse,' said her friend.

'Worse? But I thought the doctor told you yesterday that he was getting much better?'

'He did, but now today he tells me poor Ben has gone and got the convalescence.'

"*Sorry nurse, he's just been phased out.*"

Graffito on wall of teaching hospital lavatory:
  VD is nothing to clap about.

An elderly man whose cough worried nursing staff when
he was admitted for a minor operation, was sent for an
X-ray which revealed the presence of a sixpence lodged in
one of his lungs. Further investigations revealed that the
man had swallowed the coin eighteen years earlier while
enjoying a portion of Christmas pudding.

'It looks as if my husband will be in hospital for some
time,' said one neighbour to another.
  'Why, have you seen the doctors?'
  'No . . . I've seen the nurses.'

PATIENT: I don't want to get well in a hurry.
NURSE: Why not?
PATIENT: Because I'm in love with you.
NURSE: Don't worry, you won't be out that quickly.
          The doctor's in love with me too, and he's seen
          you eyeing me.'

A couple of young doctors were walking through a ward
when they noticed a patient sweating profusely. They
both put their hands under the bedclothes to take his
pulse, but by mistake got hold of each other's hands.
  'Feels like an alcoholic to me,' commented one of them.
  'I agree,' said the other.

Definition of a drug: A substance that when injected into a
guinea-pig produces a scientific paper.

Two men were lying in adjoining beds in a blood
transfusion centre discussing London. One had lived in

65

the city all his life, the other had recently arrived and didn't think much of the place. His neighbour was horrified and started trying to convince him how lucky he was living in such a unique city.

'Well, it's easy for you to talk,' scoffed the new arrival, 'you're a full-blooded Londoner.'

'No, I ain't—I'm a pint short, just like you.'

PRETTY NURSE: Every time I take this patient's pulse it gets faster and faster. What can I do?

SISTER: Blindfold him!

'The subject here limps because one leg is shorter than the other,' remarked a consultant to a group of medical students under his tuition. Turning to one of them, he asked, 'What would you do in a case like this?'

The student thought for a moment before replying, 'I think that under those circumstances, I would probably limp too.'

Graffito in a casualty department:
  Orthopaedists get all the breaks.

SURGEON: From my observation, you've got acute appendicitis, Miss Thomas.
PATIENT: I'll thank you to keep remarks like that to yourself. I came here to be cured—not admired.

An Arizona man was admitted to a hospital in the state capital, Phoenix, with gunshot wounds in one foot. After treatment for his injuries he was visited by the police who were anxious to discover how he had received them. The patient told them they were self-inflicted, though he had an explanation. Apparently he had noticed a spider walking across his foot while he was in the bathroom and unable to lay his hand on anything with which to swat it, he was forced to reach for his shotgun and give the spider both barrels.

The leaflet describing the various hoods worn by holders of degrees from Cambridge University described that of a Bachelor of Veterinary Medicine as being similar to the hood for a Bachelor of Medicine, but with more fur.

The late Lord Platt recalled the great Irish physiologist, Sir Joseph Barcroft, who devoted much of his career to the study of haemoglobin, and developed more than a passing interest in the spleen as a result. At the time little was known about this organ and when a nervous student, asked by Barcroft to outline its functions during an oral exam, finally admitted: 'I'm afraid, sir, I've forgotten', Barcroft answered: 'Good Lord, now *nobody* knows.'

Some time later, he opened a lecture to the Medico-Chirurgical Society at Sheffield on the subject of the spleen, with the announcement: 'Ladies and gentlemen, with the exception of the penis, the spleen alters its size more than any other organ of the body.'

PATIENT: I knew I wasn't dead because I was hungry and my feet were cold.
DOCTOR: What does that prove?
PATIENT: If I'd gone to Heaven I wouldn't have been hungry, and if I hadn't, my feet wouldn't have been cold.

After a detailed examination of a recently-admitted patient, a young houseman had to admit that he couldn't find the exact cause of the man's complaint, but added that it was probably due to heavy drinking.

'That's all right,' said the man cheerfully, 'I'll come back when your head's a bit clearer.'

PATIENT: Doctor, you've cured my hearing. Everything's as clear as a bell now.

DOCTOR: I'm so pleased. That will be twenty-five guineas.

PATIENT: Pardon?

An 11 year-old boy who used both his glass eye and its spare to play marbles, and lost them both during a run of poor form, was given a replacement by the National Health Service.

A former German army officer was admitted to a Bonn hospital with skin infections in various parts of his chest. When examined, he explained to doctors that these were caused by wearing his medals pinned to his naked chest. Having served in the army both during and after the Second World War, the officer, now retired, had found civvy street hard to adjust to. His wife confirmed his story, telling doctors that he wore the Iron Cross and other decorations in bed and even hoisted a flag in the bedroom.

DOCTOR: And how is your new hearing-aid working, Mrs Jones?

PATIENT: Half-past four.

At the end of a first-aid course one of the students was asked: 'Imagine that you came across a car accident and found a man lying in the road bleeding badly from a gash in his arm. What would you do?'

'Give him some brandy,' said the man without hesitation.

'And what if you hadn't any?' asked the examiner, keen to give a second chance.

'In that case I'd promise him some,' came the answer.

An elderly Sydney man who, in spite of wearing a hearing-aid for twenty-five years, had become increasingly harder of hearing, visited his local hospital to see if anything could be done to help him. In the course of the examination, the doctor removed the hearing-aid and when replacing it, accidently popped it in the other ear. The moment he did this, perfect clarity returned, and the patient heard properly for the first time in a quarter of a century—ever since the ear-piece was originally fitted to the wrong ear.

PROFESSOR: Now, assuming that you were called in to attend a patient who had swallowed a coin, what would be your method of extraction?

MEDICAL STUDENT: I'd send for a parson, sir, they can get money out of anyone.

Graffito from a London teaching hospital:
Old professors never die, they just lose their faculties.

Graffito on hospital wall:
Old doctors never die, they just lose their patients.

SORRY, WRONG LEG

Mishaps in medicine occur as often as in any other field. Of course, the public don't always hear of them, and even if you keep your ear close to the professional ground you are likely to be deafened by the rattle of closing ranks.

Now and again, however, stories do crop up. Take the case of the girl with flu who was told by her doctor to stay in bed until he called again. He forgot to come back, and she lay bed-ridden for forty years.

Not long ago a teaching hospital installed a computer to interview patients visiting its Gynaecology Department. One of the questions it asked was 'Are you having your monthly period now?' If the answer was 'yes', the computer would send the woman away and make a new appointment—in four weeks' time.

Think about it.

A French railway worker was admitted to a hospital in eastern France to have his haemorrhoids removed and left after an operation to straighten his nose instead. The surgeon who had been responsible for this oversight was fined £150 in spite of pleading in mitigation, 'It struck me that the middle of his nose was bent.'

From a manual on surgery:
Contusions of the larynx may be caused by blows or kicks, by garotting, or by a cart-wheel having passed across the neck. The affected parts are sometimes painful and there may be alteration or loss of voice.

Between 1920 and 1951 the eminent Russian physician, Serge Voronoff, grafted chimpanzees' testicles on to elderly men no fewer than 160 times. When asked to contribute an entry to the *Encyclopaedia Britannica* on 'Rejuvenation', Dr Voronoff wrote: 'The only remedy for ageing is to graft a young testicle, whether that of a human being or of an ape.' His essay made only one appearance in the encyclopaedia.

Having learned to cope with imperfect hearing in one ear since his early childhood, a Somerset man made an astonishing recovery when visiting his doctor in much later life. In the course of the examination, the doctor removed a small cork from the patient's right ear. This had been put inside the ear when the man was a child more than fifty years before.

Before public health legislation got around to restricting the flow of raw sewage into rivers, Queen Victoria paid a visit to Cambridge and remarked on the many pieces of paper she saw floating down the Cam as she was touring Trinity. 'Those, Your Majesty,' replied the Master, 'are notices warning that bathing is forbidden.'

"Oops!"

A court in California awarded damages of a quarter of a million dollars to a woman from Huntingdon Beach after 'an improperly administered enema' caused permanent lung damage.

When Harry Mills, a credit manager with a large garage chain in Dayton, Ohio discovered that he had a bare three months to live, he set about making the most of his final days. He began by appropriating 20,000 dollars from his firm which he used to throw wild parties, dine in expensive restaurants and squander as recklessly as he had always wanted to. For a time everything went well, but gradually Harry started questioning the wisdom of what he was doing. It wasn't that he didn't enjoy having a good time, the trouble was that far from starting to feel worse as his three months drew to an end, he was feeling better every day. So he decided to spend what was left of the money on a second opinion, and discovered from another doctor that he was suffering from nothing more than a simple hernia, a far cry from Crohn's disease which he'd been led to believe was about to carry him into the next world. This unfortunate error in diagnosis appeared to have been caused by the gloves worn by the surgeon who had made the exploratory examination; Harry Mills had been allergic to these, a condition that had resulted in a series of unfortunate misunderstandings all round. So instead of ending up in the great unknown, he found himself in court and given a suspended sentence on the condition that he repaid the money over the next four years.

Twenty-eight members of a New Zealand weight-watchers club suffered the indignity of having their bus sink up to its wheel-hubs in a tarred car park when they returned to it after a day out in the sun.

Soon after the opening of the Spanish shooting season, a doctor in Tarrasa was called to attend to one of the numerous casualties that occur at that time of year. On this occasion he found his patient in a tree, where he had been trying to lure birds within range by imitating their calls. The birds had stubbornly ignored him, though he did achieve a significant success with the less finely tuned ear of the crackshot who bagged him.

The staff at a seaside nursing home were at a loss to explain why one of their patients always passed water every time the local lifeboat was called out. Extensive clinical research finally provided the answer. It appeared that the electronic emptying devices attached to his partially paralyzed bladder worked on the same wavelength as the lifeboat's radio.

A middle-aged patient who had recently had her frown-line filled with liquid silicone, awoke one morning to discover that the filler had moved. Horrified, she peered into her mirror and found that her nose now stretched all the way across her eyelids and was wider by an inch around the nostrils.

Note in a retirement schedule:

If you are absent from work owing to illness or injury on the date on which you join the Plan (or, if this is a non-working day, then on the next succeeding working day) you will not be entitled to the death benefit until you return to work.

Outlining some of the problems faced in their work, a spokesman for the African Family Planning Association

"I'm sorry, but according to the autopsy, he's not dead yet."

commented: 'We are having a lot of trouble with pregnancy in secondary school girls, and this represents a lot of man-hours wasted.'

The extraordinary powers of Uri Geller extended beyond his apparent ability to bend knives and spoons without touching them—according to a Swedish girl who threatened to take him to court because of her unwanted pregnancy. Not that Mr Geller had been anywhere near her at the time. The lady claimed that his unusual force had bent the contraceptive device she had been wearing as she and her fiancé made love while watching him on television.

A chiropodist who moved into new first-floor premises found himself bankrupt less than a year later. Explaining his predicament to the court hearing his insolvency case, he said that he had forgotten that people with foot trouble are reluctant to climb stairs.

Two girls sharing a flat in London came home one night escorted by the young men with whom they had spent a riotous evening. The elder girl shrewdly offered her young friend a contraceptive device, which she eagerly accepted. The next morning, after the men had left, the elder flat-mate asked how the other had got on. 'Fine' she said, beaming, 'but that thing you gave me tasted horrible.'

An exhibition designed to recruit blood donors, and scheduled to be shown in cinemas showing the latest Dracula *film, was withdrawn after complaints from existing blood donors that it wasn't in the best taste.*

In 1936 a New York dentist gave a general anaesthetic to one of his lady patients and suddenly found her gripping his testicles with all her strength. After frantic struggles the dentist managed to free himself, but not without cost. The patient successfully sued him for 500 dollars, because he had broken one of her fingers in trying to set himself free.

In 1830, 680 Londoners watched attentively while a tumour, reputedly weighing half a hundredweight, was cut from a Chinese patient.

Having travelled all the way from Canton, the patient was spared the rigours of the return journey by his summary demise. Commenting on his death, the surgeons made no mention of the fact that the operation had lasted two hours and had been performed without anaesthetic. Indeed, they counted it a technical success, only blaming his passing away on the foulness of the air, 'poisoned' by the crowd of spectators.

The otherwise promising career of a Greek doctor working in Naples came to an abrupt halt when he was visited by a fellow countryman as a patient, who noticed that the certificate on the wall, which the doctor's Italian patients assumed was his medical diploma, was in fact a document issued by the Greek merchant navy.

Two German motorists were admitted to hospital suffering from head injuries after the ultimate in head-on collisions one foggy morning. With visibility down to a matter of feet, both drivers had been moving down the carriageway at a snail's pace, with their heads stuck out of their windows to follow the lines in the centre of the road, when they met face to face.

A 56 year-old Pole, who had lived in Britain since the war, died at his home in Stoke-on-Trent one night when he choked to death on the clove of garlic he always put in his mouth to ward off vampires while he slept.

"It's only us ma'om—come to wish you a Merry Christmas."

Traditional Greek medicine advised doctors to cure their patients of dropsy by cutting off their heads, turning their bodies upside down to drain off the offending liquids and then replacing the head to complete the recovery.

In 1978 the Australian Safety Committee, dedicated to the prevention of careless accidents, organized a marathon bed push from Hobart in Tasmania to Perth in Western Australia. A team of nurses volunteered to push a hospital bed over this 2,000 mile distance, but regrettably in the course of the journey, one of the pushers fell under the bed and received serious injuries from its castors.

A Belgian doctor who claimed to have developed a rejuvenation technique was charged with clinical malpractice and sentenced to eighteen months behind bars, in spite of his persistent claims that as a result of experimenting on himself, he was certain to live for a thousand years. This turned out to be some way short of the mark. As sentence was pronounced, the doctor collapsed with a heart attack and was rushed, unconscious, to the intensive care unit of the nearest hospital.

According to the World Health Organization in May 1975, malaria had been 'licked' and the campaign to combat it was accordingly scaled down. The announcement proved to be a little premature, for on the very afternoon it was made, the organization's Deputy General was admitted to a Geneva hospital suffering from suspected malaria.

A curry, innocently eaten at lunch-time, was blamed for the pink substance that seeped through the skin of a secretary employed by a firm in Darlington. The company's medical officer, who made a number of tests on the unfortunate victim, concluded: 'This was a phenomenon I had never come across before. Something in her system reacted against turmeric in the curry and sent something like pink dye through her pores.'

A century ago Sigmund Freud had this to say about white powder extracted from the cocoa leaf: 'Exhilaration and lasting euphoria, which in no way differs from the normal euphoria of a healthy person . . . You perceive an increase in self-control and possess more vitality and capacity for work. In other words, you are simply more normal, and it is soon hard to believe that you are under the influence of any drug.'
And the name of this remarkable substance? We call it cocaine.

A man accused of breaking into a contraceptive machine appeared before magistrates to explain his behaviour and told them: 'It was our wedding night and my wife wouldn't let me get into bed until I had a contraceptive. Unfortunately neither of us had any change.'

Among the regulations governing the leave taken from work by certain employees of the US government, was the following humane paragraph:

When an employee absent from duty on account of illness dies without making application for advanced sick leave, the fact of death is sufficient to show a 'serious disability' and to dispense with the requirement of a formal application and a medical certificate.

Until comparatively recently it was seriously believed that disease could be conquered by noise. During an outbreak of cholera in London in 1832, a dentist put forward the idea that the city should be ringed with artillery firing hourly round the clock.

"Looks like some kind of tribal health warning . . ."

The hazardous business of medical research has carried off at least two eminent British writers. On 9th April, 1626, Francis Bacon ate a goose stuffed with snow, to see whether this primitive method of deep-freezing had preserved the bird's flesh. The author of *The Advancement of Learning* soon discovered that it hadn't and died of typhoid as a result.

Just over three hundred years later, Arnold Bennett succumbed to the same disease in Paris after drinking a glass of water in an attempt to prove that Parisian water was perfectly safe to drink.

The brilliant Scottish physician, Dr John Hunter, managed to give himself syphilis in the course of trying to prove that it and gonorrhoea were one and the same disease. After deliberately infecting himself with what he took to be gonorrhoea, he carefully studied the development of the disease which first became apparent with, in his own words 'a teasing itching in those parts'. This developed along the classic lines of syphilis and seemed to confirm Hunter's theory. Unfortunately the donor of the pus with which Hunter infected himself had in fact been suffering from syphilis all along and the good doctor eventually died as a result of this oversight.

A father trying to force open his children's money-box cut himself so badly in the process that he was forced to spend the contents on lint and bandages.

A Swedish man whose finances took a turn for the worse in 1910, sold his body to one of Stockholm's leading hospitals, to be used for medical research after his death.

The deal was signed, the fee for the use of the body paid over and all was well, until an unexpected legacy dramatically improved the donor's bank balance. He resolved to reclaim the rights to his body and asked the hospital if he could buy it back. They refused; fought their case in court and won possession of the man's body. To add insult to injury, they also obtained damages because the man had had a couple of teeth removed without first asking their permission as legal owners of his body.

A sixteenth-century Jewish doctor is credited with having performed one of the earliest blood transfusions on the ailing Pope Innocent VIII. Selecting three healthy boys as donors, the doctor set about his work. Of the five participants, however, only one survived this medical breakthrough—and that was the doctor.

While grasping the principles of infection, medieval doctors still came unstuck on some of the finer points of detail. Henry VIII's venereal disease, for example, was attributed to Cardinal Wolsey and the fact that he had been incautious enough to whisper in the king's ear.

During the Great Plague of 1665 one prescription on sale to the terrified citizens of London specified 'the brains of a young man that hath died a violent death, together with its membranes, arteries, veins, nerves, and all the pith of the backbone, bruising these in a stone mortar 'till they become a kind of pap, then putting in as much of spirits of wine as will cover the breadth of three fingers, and digesting for a year in horse dung'. This medicine was to be taken twice daily with water!

In 1963, the NHS printed a form laying down instructions for applicants seeking supplementary eye services, which was unreadable to anyone who needed glasses.

Following the birth of their second child, Mr and Mrs Alf Lincoln decided to call a halt. In November 1977 Mrs Lincoln went into hospital for a hysterectomy. Eighteen months later she went into hospital again—to give birth to a bouncing baby boy.

While working on the extension to a hospital in the Mozambique capital Maputo, workmen demolished a wall and found a fully-equipped maternity ward that had apparently been mislaid by the hospital authorities. Internal enquiries revealed that the original contractors erected a wall instead of a door, but that didn't explain why no one had missed the ward during the seven years of the hospital's operation.

After spending five days in a Los Angeles hospital for treatment of an eye infection, a California man was sent a bill for three hundred dollars for the delivery of a baby. 'Please correct the error,' he wrote back, 'or at least send me the baby.'

"Hargreaves—GMC—plain-clothes division!"

Advertisement in a medical journal:
Surgical instruments for sale: complete assortment of deceased surgeons.

Doctor: No, nurse! I told you to prick his boil . . .

In 1979 a 42 year-old lady executive was awarded damages of 854,000 dollars by a court in New York after an operation to flatten her stomach which resulted in shifting her tummy button two inches off centre.

Distinguished Company . . .
PERSONAL CONTRIBUTIONS

Now here are some reports from the blunt end of the stethoscope.

Even well-known people get ill from time to time. W. C. Fields, a devout non-believer, was found towards the end of his life reading the Bible in his sick-bed. His explanation? 'Looking for loop-holes.'

The managing director of a large company once showed me a letter he received in hospital. It came from his company secretary, and read: 'Your colleagues on the Board have asked me to send you good wishes for your speedy recovery. This motion was passed by twelve votes to eleven.'

Here I would like to make an appeal. A certain lady is mentioned in Leslie Crowther's reminiscence, and if she happens to read this book, I would be fascinated to hear from her what it was she saw that made her say what she did . . .

LESLIE CROWTHER—*Caught with his pants down*

After having had my varicose veins done in 1969, I was swathed in bandages from my pelvis to my ankles, apart from the naughty bits, for ten days. At the end of that time the bandages were removed, so that the stitches could be taken out. This necessitated my lying flat on my back, stark naked, while the nurses bent over my embarrassed body and worked away.

As I was lying there, trying to think of other things, like dead dogs and grandmothers, the matron came in. She always chose her moments with great care. 'Mr Crowther,' she said, 'my secretary is a great fan of yours and would love to meet you.'

Thinking that then was as good a time as any, I told her to come in. 'Miss White,' the matron called, and Miss White burst into the room on a tide of excited chatter, saying, 'Mr Crowther, I've been a great fan of yours for as long as I can . . . oh, my goodness!' Then she turned puce and started talking even more excitedly, though this time with less sense, as she scanned me lying full-length and barefooted to my chin. Finally she got control of the situation and backed out of the room as she said, 'Mr Crowther, it's been lovely meeting you. And, you know, we don't see nearly enough of you on the telly!'

RONNIE BARKER—*Disorderly conduct*

In 1949, I worked as an orderly for six months at the Wingfield Hospital in Oxford, where, for some reason, I was known as Charlie, and was mainly celebrated for my skills with the bedpan. Empty ones I would play like a banjo, and full ones would be slid across the ward's polished floor, using the feet, rather like a cross between the Scottish game of curling, and football. My finest hour was when I sent a pan whizzing across the floor and it sailed between the legs of the ward sister—the first time that anything had done so for years, I was informed later.

I've got a favourite old medical joke too:
'Excuse me, how do I get to the hospital?'
'Stand in the middle of the road and shout: 'Three cheers for the Kaiser.'

EAMONN ANDREWS—*Tubular consultations*

I have a doctor who's a very good doctor and, like all very good doctors, he can tell almost as much at a glance as he can after thumping and poking and peering and listening. I speak, of course, as one of those lucky ones who has been blessed with rude good health for the most part. Nevertheless, as time goes on, you tend to need reassurance that this, that and the other are working well enough to keep the Great Reaper at a disinterested distance.

This is where my medical conscience bothers me—occasionally. Since my job means regular appearance on television, my medical guru takes the occasional look and, no doubt, mutters to himself 'Andrews looks O.K.' So, when I call him for a consultation, I'm as likely to be told: 'You're fine. Don't worry. I checked you last night.'

I don't mention anything about fees. Think I'm mean not to suggest he drops me a little bill for, say, tubular consultations?

This saves a lot of time with the dentist, too. To get full value here, however, I'd have to arrange the occasional yawn—not as easy, you may say, for those looking out as for those looking in!

*"To ... er ... recap, your excellency—you think you're
N. J. Wickley of 16, Beech Terrace, Cricklewood?"*

PAUL EDDINGTON—*Too many chiefs ...*

A friend of mine, travelling in India, was stricken with
an acute appendicitis. Rushed to hospital, he was
given a general anaesthetic and taken to the theatre.
Unfortunately, he regained consciousness before he
should have done, to hear one of the surgeons saying
angrily to the other: 'Mr Rajahgopalachari! Who is in
charge of this operation—you or me?'

He says it was a very alarming experience.

FRANKIE HOWERD—*Inside knowledge*

A patient came round in a hospital recovery ward after an operation to see what was going on inside him, and exclaimed with relief: 'Thank goodness that's over!'

'I wouldn't be too sure if I were you,' said the man in the bed next to him. 'They left a swab in me and had to do it all over again to get it out.'

'And they had to cut me open too,' added the man in the bed on the other side. 'They'd lost one of their forceps.'

At that moment the surgeon who had operated on the patient who had just regained consciousness popped his head round the door and asked, 'Has anyone seen my hat?'

His patient fainted.

ROBERT DOUGALL—*Doctor at sea*

This is one of those funny peculiar happenings during a wartime Arctic convoy from Scapa to Murmansk. I was then a raw sub-lieutenant taking passage in the escort destroyer *HMS Savage*. One morning a merchant ship in the convoy came alongside and requested over the loudhailer that our doctor should go aboard to attend a case of appendicitis. Unfortunately, *Savage* was due to take on oil and the Captain was reluctant to waste any time, especially as he knew a U-boat pack was in the offing. Accordingly, our medical officer was told to confine himself to giving advice over the loudhailer; this he did, with talk of hot water bottles and so on. Afterwards, the Doc had strong words to say about not being allowed to visit a patient, but there was nothing further he could do.

By the next day, the U-boats were awaiting the convoy south of Bear Island. The attack came in the blackness. For a time it was total confusion. *Savage* put down a pattern of depth charges; there was an almighty explosion and wreckage of all kinds floated past. At first we thought we'd got a U-boat; soon there were rafts with oil-covered figures all around us. We realized then that they were Americans and managed to pick up fifty-one survivors from that luckless Liberty ship; what's more, it was the very ship with the appendicitis case and he, amazingly,

was one of those fished out of the icy sea. So, the patient had finally come to the Doc instead of the other way round.

The tragic irony of it all was that a medical officer from one of the other escort destroyers, who had been allowed to board the merchantman, went down with the ship.

Imagine my amazement thirty years later, in 1974, when as the victim of 'This Is Your Life', I was confronted with the former appendicitis case, a Texan now living in a suburb of New York, blithely walking into the Thames Television Studio. Heaven knows how the programme researchers had managed to track him down.

His name, not inappropriately, was A. C. Hazard.

JAMES HERRIOT—*Sedatives natural and narcotic*

One of the irritating little problems in veterinary practice is dealing with the sow which savages its young. Certain animals, clearly lacking in maternal instinct, will attack their piglets as soon as they are born and will not allow them to suckle.

At the present time we have various sedative drugs to quieten the mother, so that she will accept her litter, but thirty years ago the vets were still groping in the dark and willing to try out anything which the pharmaceutical companies produced.

In the early 'fifties I was called to a sow which was exhibiting these unfortunate symptoms and I had just taken delivery of a new injection which I had been assured would solve the problem. I went eagerly to the case, full of youthful enthusiasm, and as I inserted my needle in the pig, I told the farmer that the new drug would definitely do the trick.

I did indeed feel confident because the sales talk promoting the injection had been very convincing, but after a long wait the big sow was still barking angrily at her piglets and refusing to allow them near her.

I was ready to give up, when the farmer's old father took a hand. He sent down to the local pub for a bucketful of their best bitter beer and poured it into the pig's trough. The animal drank deeply and with obvious enjoyment, and within a short time she was laid out blissfully on her side with her family sucking happily at her teats.

It was embarrassing for me, but it was not the only time that home-spun remedies had triumphed over my so-called science.

"Oh, I'd love to be in your next film, but surely you can't both be Richard Gordon."

PAUL DANIELS—*Doctor, Doctor*

PATIENT: Doctor, Doctor, I keep thinking I am invisible.
DOCTOR: Who said that?

PATIENT: Doctor, Doctor, I keep thinking I am a pair of curtains.
DOCTOR: Oh, pull yourself together, man.

PATIENT: Doctor, Doctor, I keep thinking that I'm a hen.
DOCTOR: Take these pills, and if they don't cure you, I'll have two dozen eggs.

PATIENT: Doctor, Doctor, I keep thinking people are ignoring me.
DOCTOR: Next please!

GAYLE HUNNICUTT—*Hair today and gone tomorrow*

I have always been lucky in having quite thick hair, which I have come to rely on as a flattering frame for my face. Therefore, it came as quite a shock when I noticed it was starting to thin out rather drastically. This was brought abruptly to my attention when I went to meet a friend for lunch and was greeted by the exclamation: 'What has happened to your hair?' My heart froze, and while I mumbled some inconsequential reply, I made a mental note to see a trichologist as soon as possible.

He quickly put my mind at rest, explaining that I wasn't going bald, but simply suffering from a metabolic shock to the system. Apparently this had been caused by my having stopped taking a thyroid prescription, which I'd been clinging to for years in the vague idea that it helped to keep my weight down. Only a change of house and doctors revealed that not only was this medication unnecessary, but it was actually making me maintain a higher weight level due to its metabolic upheaval in my body. As a side effect it was also encouraging my hair to fall out.

It wasn't long before it started to grow back again, aided by a course of treatment at the clinic; but it was almost a close shave, in more ways than one.

"You know, if it wasn't for you chaps coming over here, our health service would collapse."

MIRIAM KARLIN—*'This is truly my first hospital experience'*

Whilst still in my teens, I was admitted to hospital with appendicitis. The night before the op, the anaesthetist came to visit me with a cigarette hanging out of his mouth and carrying a very full ashtray, which he placed on my tummy. He then took out his stethoscope, gave me the routine examination, and said: 'All right, I'll see you in the morning.'

He was already out of the door when I called out: 'Hey—haven't you forgotten something?'

Puzzled, he said: 'No . . . no . . . I don't think so. I've got my ashtray . . .', whereupon I threw his stethoscope after him.

I still wonder to this day how many Woodbines are floating about my innards!

DEREK NIMMO—*On noses*

In spite of all appearances to the contrary, I was born with a singularly straight and pleasant nose, which remained with me throughout early childhood until I joined the Wolf Cubs. There, soon after my recruitment, I was tripped up by my senior sixer, landed on my nose and developed a large lump on it which remained there until I landed my first theatre job at the Hippodrome, Bolton.

Owing to this curious lump on my nose, I found myself being cast mainly in rather sinister roles; I particularly remember the director advising me to specialize in baby-faced killers. This seemed to be a fairly limited market and my mother prevailed on me to have the offending lump cut off.

Since Robert Donat was a particular favourite of my mother's, I took a photograph of him in profile with me when I went to Stoke Mandeville Hospital in Aylesbury, then, as now, one of the leading centres of plastic surgery in the country.

The surgeon was very kind and accommodating and arranged for me to be popped in to have my nose seen to. The bandages stayed in place for several days after the operation until, with mounting excitement, they were finally removed. Then it had to be admitted that things had gone a trifle awry. In a fit of enthusiasm, too much of the nose had been cut away and, as any snapshot will now show, it turned up at the end rather like a ski-jump. My career as a second Robert Donat was brought to a sudden halt and I was forced to play comedy ever since.

The good doctor was frightfully apologetic and very kindly offered to slip me in again to graft a bit of bone off my hip and on to my nose to straighten things out. At the time I really couldn't face another operation; but I have never forgotten his kind offer. There's always the reassurance that if ever my luck in comedy runs out, I can go back and have the bone shifted from hip to nose, even if it means that thereafter I'll be forced to play villains with limps!

"You paid the pusher by selling my manuscripts to Conan who?!"

MAGGIE PHILBIN—*Facts of life*

One of my parents' fondest memories of me as a seven-year-old occurred whilst driving in the car. We'd just visited some friends whose dog had produced a litter of puppies. I had been sitting quietly in the back seat for about fifteen minutes when I piped up with 'I know why our dog hasn't had puppies.' My parents froze, wondering what was to follow. 'We're giving her the wrong type of dog biscuits,' I added brightly.

KENNETH WILLIAMS—*Tall tales*

When I was in hospital in 1974 there was this garrulous night nurse who told me she'd ticked off an elderly incontinent patient about the state of the bed, and the old lady had replied: 'Rubbish! It's the roof leaking, you fool!' I murmured something about the ingenious excuse, and she added: 'That's nothing! When I asked her about the soiled sheet on another day, she told me it was iron-mould!' I smiled at the implausibility of that, but my expression changed when she confided: 'We had that Idi Amin in the operating theatre for the haemorrhoidals! We had to roll him in flour to find out where his arse was!'

MAGNUS PYKE—*National health and how to run it*

As one of the scientists behind the scheme to protect the health of the British public during the years of World War II, by making a concentrate of vitamin C out of rose hips, I was deputed to serve on the Vegetable Drugs Committee of the Ministry of Health. This committee, under the chairmanship of Sir Weldon Dalrymple Champneys, had the responsibility of organizing the preparation of all sorts of drugs from native plants and herbs. At each meeting, when my turn came, I had to report the tonnage of rose hips that had been collected. The Committee then authorized the release of the appropriate quantity of sugar needed to turn the hips into syrup. Membership of this committee was an education to me in the art of civil service administration. For example, there was always an item on the agenda relating to the collection of horse chestnuts. As far as I could gather, these were used for the manufacture of Lucozade as a sustaining beverage for convalescents. The tonnage collected was impressive. Far down the table, however, a member of the committee reported to Sir Weldon that the sacks issued by the Ministry of Supply were, when full, so heavy that several of the volunteer lady collectors had ruptured themselves lifting them. Could there be an issue of half-hundredweight sacks? Sir Weldon instructed the secretary of the committee to look into the matter and report at the next meeting.

You listening, Doc? OK. Six o'clock tonight you go to the park and make sure you're not followed. Fifteen yards due south of the ornamental fish pond you'll find the hollow tree. Look inside the tree and you'll find your Merit Award.

The war went on; the bombs dropped; the committee met once more and the secretary reported. The Ministry of Supply had considered the problem. They were, owing to current shortages, unable to issue the half-hundredweight sacks. They had, however, prepared a circular instructing those involved in the collection of horse chestnuts only to fill the hundredweight sacks half full.

My education continued. At each meeting, a certain group of collectors was congratulated on having increased the tonnage of stinging nettles gathered in to help the war effort. I asked my neighbour what was the purpose of this particular activity. He did not know. Although it was no business of mine, I could not forbear asking the Chairman. He turned to the secretary. 'Why do we collect stinging nettles?' 'I am sorry, Sir Weldon, but I am not permitted to say.'

Meetings followed one another as the war progressed and the battle-front ebbed and flowed. Devoted collectors gathered in the nettles in ever-increasing amounts. There came a time when I asked again the purpose of this bizarre, and not altogether painless, proceeding. 'Is it yet possible, Sir Weldon, to divulge what use is made of them?' Again he referred to the secretary, who coughed in obvious embarrassment.

'Actually, Chairman,' he said, 'the original request came from the War Office who proposed to use them as a source of chlorophyll. Our Intelligence had discovered that German pilots had been issued with tinted spectacles which enabled them to recognize the green dye with which the camouflage nets designed to conceal our gun batteries were coloured. It was proposed, therefore, to dye the nets with chlorophyll, the colour of which possesses the same spectral make-up as the surrounding foliage. Unfortunately,' he coughed again, 'it seems that it was not found possible to prevent the chlorophyll being affected by rain and, in fact, Sir Weldon, for some time now the nettle collections have not actually been used.'

IRENE THOMAS—*A few ancient jests ...*

... ranging from the wry one-liner first heard during the 1939–45 war:

One army MO to another: 'What were you in civilian life?'
... to the answer given by the doctor to an anxious patient:

'What is it? ... Well, it's rather rare, but the last time I saw it the whole herd had to be put down.'

Or the one in similar vein (Ho! Ho!) ...

DOCTOR: Do you get green spots before the eyes ... ? And a purple rash ... ? And red stripes on the tongue ... ?
PATIENT: Y-y-yes ...
DOCTOR: So do I. I wonder what it is?

My favourite is the rather cynical one about the two surgeons chatting in their club:

'I hear you operated on old Carruthers last week ... what for?'
'Five hundred guineas.'
'No, I mean what did he have?'
'Five hundred guineas.'

110

"You must have got it wrong, Benson—he can't seriously be complaining of greenfly . . ."

ROBERT ROBINSON—*With acknowledgement to the repertoire of Dr Michael O'Donnell*

The surgeon was completing his examination of an elderly party, and pointing to the old fellow's testicles, cried (in the breezy way surgeons seem to specialize in): 'Those are going to have to come off.'

'Dear me,' (or words to that effect) muttered the patient.

'After all,' said the surgeon, booming cheerfully away, 'they're no use to you.'

The elderly party looked thoughtfully at the surgeon. 'No,' he said, 'but they *are* rather showy . . .'

FRED TRUEMAN—*Last request*

An 85 year-old patient named Alice, whilst being attended by her doctors, informed them that she had one dying ambition. When they asked what this was, she astonished them by saying she wanted to 'do a streak'. The doctors were more than a little taken aback, but after due consultation one of them offered the opinion, 'At her age I don't think she's likely to do any harm or damage to herself or anyone else.' Permission was therefore granted.

Alice jumped out of bed, whipped off her nightdress and set off to fulfil her ambition. She streaked through Ward 4, Wards 5 and 6, down the corridor, through the reception doors and across the lawn. Sitting on a seat were two elderly gentlemen patients, smoking their pipes. As she flashed past, one removed his pipe and said: 'Did you see what I saw?' 'Yes,' replied his friend, 'it looked like old Alice from Ward 3.'

The other chap said, 'That's what I thought. I don't know what she was wearing, but it certainly wanted ironing.'

JULIE WALTERS—*People remember nurses*

During one of my spells of duty as a night nurse I had to admit a patient who had been due to arrive during the day, but who finally showed up at around midnight. He was quite elderly and very deaf which didn't make my job any easier as I tried to get him into bed without disturbing the other patients fast asleep in the ward.

To add to my troubles, the consultant on this ward always required a mid-stream urine specimen from new arrivals. We had special packs for these consisting of a small tin-foil container, into which went a mild disinfectant, a container for the specimen and some cotton wool balls. The idea was that the patients used the cotton wool and disinfectant to clean their 'parts', then started to pee and caught some mid-stream, as it were.

Trying to explain this to my new arrival was rather difficult, so I took him down to the ward toilets to avoid waking the others. He nodded blankly as I started to demonstrate what the pack was for and when it was clear that he still didn't understand, I tried to do it for him— well, at least clean his 'winkie' for him. But when he saw me bending down to his flies with the cotton wool ball in my fingers, he backed away frantically and became quite threatening. However, he got the message, banged me on the shoulders and nodded that he understood, which meant that I could leave him to it while I got on with my other duties.

It must have been a couple of hours later that I remembered the specimen. I dashed back to the toilet and found it empty except for the pack, complete apart from the disinfectant and the urine sample. The old man had found his way back to bed and was lying awake when I asked him what he'd done with it. Amid shushing from all sides, he patted me reassuringly on the shoulder again and boomed confidently: 'Yes, I drank the medicine.'

"And every time I go for a quick draw, I get this sort of twinge just there, doc."

MIKE YARWOOD—*Joking apart*

After a very difficult Caesarian operation that had taken eleven hours, everybody was exhausted.

The surgeon asked, 'Was it a boy or a girl?'

'I don't know,' replied the nurse.

'Neither do I,' said the obstetrician.

A young anaesthetist was standing by and shyly said: 'Let me see the baby . . . I know how you can tell.'

Looking at the sick man, the doctor decided to tell him the truth: 'I'm afraid you're a very ill man, but I'm sure you would want to know the facts. Now, is there anyone you would like to see?'

'Yes, another doctor,' murmured the patient feebly.

When a patient came round after his operation, he saw there were screens all round his bed.

'What's the idea of these?' he asked the nurse. 'Didn't you expect me to recover?'

'Oh, it's not that,' she said. 'It's just that the premises opposite caught fire and burst into flames while you were out, and we didn't want you to come round and think that the worst had happened.'

AND FROM THE DOCTORS THEMSELVES

It is said that the most important part of the stethoscope is the part between the ears. In this section you have a chance to sample the wit and wisdom and wickedness of the medical profession.

It is surprising how many doctors can be extremely funny— in fact those of us who can't come up to their standard have been forced out of the profession and into show business.

I was lucky enough to be a student of J. G. Yates-Bell, the urologist, and a fine teacher. He was a stickler for politeness and regard for his patients, and if a student failed to introduce himself to the gentleman he was asked to examine, Yates-Bell would enquire if it was his normal habit to approach a complete stranger and shake him warmly by the scrotum. When one of our group made the mistake of carrying out an examination with one hand in his trouser pocket, Yates-Bell stopped him cold.

'What are you doing?' he asked. 'Comparing sizes?'

MR JASON BRICE (Southampton General Hospital)

In my early days as a consultant I fancied myself as an after-dinner speaker and accepted invitations to speak at annual dinners of organizations of which I had little knowledge. On one occasion I was booked to speak after dinner at a well-known hotel on the South Coast of England. As luck would have it, I had to operate for longer than expected and therefore arrived late. At the entrance waited a very anxious and slightly exasperated speaker's secretary, who asked if I was their speaker. I answered that I was, never having met anyone from the organization I was due to address.

On my way through the foyer I glanced at a notice-board announcing that the organization I was due to address was occupying one room, and out of the corner of my eye caught sight of the words 'Sand and Gravel'—and the name of another room. My host hustled me into a large dinner where I took my seat at the head of the table and started eating while chatting animatedly to the lady and gentleman on either side. I happened to notice someone else's name on the card in front of me, but thought nothing of it, assuming that it belonged to one of my neighbours.

When my turn came to speak, the Chairman stood up and introduced me as 'an acknowledged expert on the extraction of gravel from the sea bed' and proceeded to describe my career in that profession in the most glowing

"He says he can't see you just now—he's too busy writing his oath."

terms. That was when it dawned on me that I was actually occupying the seat of the guest speaker at the wrong dinner and, more to the point, with the wrong speech. The one I delivered was a hastily concocted description of the occurrence of kidney and gall bladder stones and what I could remember of their removal from the human body. This caused some astonishment among the guests, followed, mercifully, by an equal measure of amusement.

A consultant radiologist colleague of mine was in the habit of taking a shower in the surgeons' changing-room before he went home after a long day's work. Next to the shower-room, was the room where we changed into our operating suits and on the wall was a blackboard on which the theatre sisters wrote the telephone numbers of the duty staff each evening.

121

I was in the shower after a tiring day in the theatre on one occasion, as my radiology colleague was towelling himself down after his ablutions, when the door burst open and one of the theatre sisters, clearly intent on posting the duty rota for the evening, hurried in. She beat a hasty retreat, murmuring apologies to Dr X as she left. There wasn't anything particularly unusual about this incident, but what interested me was that at the moment she burst in, my colleague's head and face had been totally swathed in his bath towel leaving only the lower half of his anatomy on view.

I felt that was a case of knowing some members of the team too well.

Back in the days when ether, that highly inflammable and explosive agent, was still widely used as an anaesthetic, there was a famous London neurosurgeon who made regular trips to a mental hospital in South Wales to perform operations. His visits were the bane of the hospital's Medical Superintendent, appropriately a Dr Wales, who invariably bore the brunt of the great man's notorious temper.

As a man of orderly habits, the neurosurgeon always retired to the lavatory before starting an operation, where he enjoyed a cigarette while completing *The Times* crossword. On the morning in question, he dropped his cigarette between his legs, as he was accustomed to do, only a fraction of a second before there was an enormous explosion, which was rapidly followed by the surgeon's voice, that could be heard throughout the hospital, bellowing 'Wales!'

The Medical Superintendent kept a low profile, though he was heard to comment that at last his distinguished visitor 'had seen the light'. Meanwhile the neurosurgeon stumbled from the wreckage of the lavatory, with a different view of the world, searching for the theatre technician who had emptied the remains of the ether bottle into the WC pan.

LADY HAMILTON (Chairman of the Disabled Living Foundation)

A doctor had a splendid tomcat, who caused a lot of trouble with the local lady cats, both with his love songs and with the kittens. As a result of forceful representations over a period, the neighbours prevailed on the doctor to take the tomcat to the vet. Luckily, the tomcat survived the operation and came back home. However, after this sad experience, the doctor was surprised to see his cat frequently on the lawn with several other cats around him obviously paying great attention. That is the end of the story, but the moral is:

If you have the knowledge and experience, but lack the necessary equipment, you are well advised to set up as a consultant.

DR WENDY GREENGROSS and DR MICHAEL HUMPHREY (St George's Hospital Medical School, London)

An elderly man, the victim of a road traffic accident, was brought into Casualty with his wife. After some time, the Casualty officer appeared and drew a blanket up over the old man's face, saying: 'I'm sorry, madam, I'm afraid he's gone.'

'No I ain't,' said a voice from under the blanket.

'Shut up, Bill,' snapped the wife, 'the doctor knows best!'

*"Well I was wrong and you were right, Mrs Nesbit—
there is a beetle crawling round in your kidney."*

DR MICHAEL O'DONNELL

In our first clinical year at St Thomas's we attended lectures in which people like Sharpey-Shafer, the professor of medicine, and his reader Tony Dornhorst tried to convince us that clinical medicine was a science and not a collection of old docs' tales. Tony Dornhorst tried to help us undertand the circulation with what he called 'an electrical analogy'. His equations, laden with symbols, were more baffling than the hydrodynamics they were supposed to simplify but we could forgive him anything because of the throwaway lines he forced through his stammer. One sleepy summer afternoon he asked a student to name the causes of an enlarged spleen. The student shook himself from half slumber and, playing for time, muttered: 'The causes are legion, sir.'

'Then just give us a co-co-cohort or two,' said Tony Dornhorst.

DR DANNIE ABSE

Physiology lectures at King's College in the Strand were made entertaining by Professor MacDowell. 'We have three instincts,' he would say, 'three instincts, gentlemen. One could call them the three Fs: Fear, Food and Reproduction.' It seemed Professor MacDowell would sometimes be consulted by patients concerned about their hearts. But that year, for reasons of wartime economy, the lifts at King's were not working and the Professor's office was high, high up, close to the roof. Thus the heart patients had to climb all those endless stone steps.

'I don't have to examine them when they reach my door,' he said. 'If they make it that proves their hearts are sound; if not, then it's just a question of writing out the death certificate.'

Later, at Westminster Hospital, I joined my first medical firm. One afternoon while the firm waited for a consultant who for some reason that day had been delayed, his registrar decided to teach us a singularly important principle of medicine. He asked a nurse to fetch him a sample of urine. He then talked to us about diabetes mellitus. '*Diabetes*,' he said, 'is a Greek name; but the Romans noticed that bees liked the urine of diabetics so they added the word *mellitus* which means sweet as honey. Well, as you know, you may find sugar in the urine of a diabetic...' By now the nurse had returned with a sample of urine which the registrar promptly held up like a trophy. We stared at that straw-coloured fluid as if we had never seen such a thing before. The registrar then startled us. He dipped a finger boldly into the urine then licked that finger with the tip of his tongue. As if tasting wine he opened and closed his lips rapidly. Could he perhaps detect a faint taste of sugar? The sample was passed on to us for an opinion. We all dipped a finger into the fluid, all of us foolishly licked that finger. 'Now,' said the registrar, grinning, 'you have learnt the first principle of diagnosis. I mean the power of observation.' We were baffled. We stood near the sluice room outside the ward and, in the distance, some anonymous patient was explosively coughing. 'You see,' the registrar continued triumphantly, 'I dipped my *middle* finger into the urine but licked my *index* finger—not like you chaps.'

"And tonight, in our discussion on transplant surgery ..."

PROFESSOR JOHN HERMON-TAYLOR (St George's Hospital Medical School, London)

Randolph Churchill was admitted to a distinguished London hospital under the care of a very eminent thoracic surgeon. The suspected diagnosis was a tumour in the left lung. The resident surgical officer was instructed to arrange the operation, which duly took place on the Wednesday of that week. Fortunately, the condition turned out not to be cancer after all, but an area of unresolved pneumonia.

Randolph's recovery was characterized only by his robust and individualistic personality, and was otherwise uncomplicated.

Later, a close member of the family was heard to remark, 'Those damned fool doctors have gone and removed the only bit of Randolph that was not malignant.'

DR EDWARD LOWBURY

We had lectures on tropical medicine from Dr Manson-Bahr, a robust personality who enlivened his discourse with reminiscences of medical practice in tropical countries. I was charmed by the account of his weekly out-patient clinic in, I believe, Cairo. Patients who had had dysentery were asked to bring a specimen of faeces with them to these clinics for laboratory examination. People used a great variety of containers for their specimens. One day he asked a patient why he had not brought a specimen, and the man replied 'I *did* bring a specimen, and it was in a sardine tin; but someone sitting next to me on the bus stole it from my pocket, and I didn't have the heart to say "Give that back!"'

A surgical teacher whom no 'Londoner' of the nineteen-thirties could ever forget was Russell Howard. He was a heavy, elderly man with a slight stoop, a scowl, a plebeian twang and a lively directness of expression. He was a stickler for punctuality. 'You're late, Mr Fletcher,' he snapped as a student came into the lecture room. 'Detained at stool, sir,' chirped Fletcher; to which R.H. fired back 'Well, Mr Fletcher, since surgical out-patients I bin and 'ad tea with Sister Gloucester *and* passed me water and got 'ere in time.'

He often shot questions on anatomy at us, and complained of our ignorance. 'And where's Poupart's

Junction?' Someone started 'Where the inguinal ligament...' but was cut short with a stentorian 'Nonsense; it's about a mile out of Waterloo Station!'

"Don't be silly. He's far too little to carry a case of anything—let alone rabies."

DR OLIVER PRATT (Institute of Psychiatry, London)

The regional hospital was a good, solid Victorian structure. Half-hidden under trees at the back was a low brick building—the original mortuary, almost unchanged and therefore rather old-fashioned. The staff who manned it were trying hard to persuade the hospital authorities to get it refitted and re-equipped.

One day several of the hospital doctors were gathered in this mortuary waiting for the pathologist to carry out a post-mortem for them. But, before he could start his investigation, a very unusual thing occurred—the 'body' flickered an eyelid and uttered a moan.

Amidst the ensuing consternation, embarrassed nurses and attendants hurried the 'corpse' back to a ward, while the senior mortuary assistant came across to the pathologist to say: 'There now, doctor—if you had bought that new deep freeze that I've been asking for to keep the bodies in, that would never have happened.'

DR S. MOSSMAN (The Royal Free Hospital, London)

A porter, more than a little hard of hearing, was given an urgent message to take the cardiac arrest trolley to Ward 13. He rushed off there to meet the impatient doctors but arrived breathlessly pushing the dinner trolley.

DR MIRIAM STOPPARD

One of my lecturers at the Royal Free Hospital who had the duty of saying grace before dinner frequently couldn't come up with the proper Latin. While we bowed our heads, he would mutter: 'Levator labii superioris alaeque nasi', which is the name of a small muscle running down the side of the nose to the upper lip.

PROFESSOR R. SMITHELLS (The General Infirmary at Leeds)

As I was walking down the children's ward in the hospital, a precocious three-year-old, standing at the foot of the cot, stopped me with a peremptory finger.
   'Who are you?' she demanded.
   I told her.
   'What are you for?' she asked.
   I have yet to think of a satisfactory answer.

MR PAUL STANDING (West Middlesex University Hospital)

The Chain of Command

From: District Superintendent
To: Superintendent
Tomorrow morning there will be a total eclipse of the sun at 0900 hours. This is something that we cannot see every day, so allow the students to line up outside in their best uniforms to watch it.

To make an occasion of this rare occurrence I will personally explain it to them.

If it is raining we shall not be able to see it very well. In that case the students should assemble in the dining-room.

*　　*　　*

From: Superintendent
To: Senior I
By order of the District Superintendent there will be a total eclipse of the sun at 9 a.m. tomorrow morning, if it is raining we shall not be able to see it on site, in our best uniforms.

In that case the disappearance of the sun will be

followed through the dining-room.

This is something that cannot be seen every day.

*   *   *

From: Senior I
To: Senior II

By order of the District Superintendent we shall follow through in our best uniforms the disappearance of the sun in the canteen at 9 o'clock tomorrow morning.

The superintendent will tell us whether it is going to rain.

This is something which we cannot see every day.

*   *   *

From: Senior II
To: Basic Grades

If it is raining in the dining-room tomorrow morning, which is something we cannot see every day, the Superintendent, in his best uniform, will disappear at 9 o'clock.

*   *   *

From: Basic Grades
To: Students

Tomorrow morning at 9 we shall see the District Superintendent disappear.

It is a pity we cannot see this happen every day.

DR WILLIAM TARNOW-MORDI (John Radcliffe
Hospital, Oxford)

Hospital telephone switchboard operators are often
admirable in the way they keep the flow of vital
information going under great stress, at all hours, despite
ramshackle equipment and impatient callers. But
sometimes they get things alarmingly wrong; like my
name for instance. Since qualifying I have been known
variously as Dr Taram Salata, Dr Tobermory and Ta no
more dear. But my favourite, being a keen devotee of soul
music, is . . . Dr Tamla Motown.

"Good God! Call yourself a patient?"

PROFESSOR P. K. THOMAS (Royal Free Hospital School of Medicine, London)

A consultant was teaching a group of medical students at the bedside. It was a hot day and he droned on interminably while the students had to stand attentively. Suddenly, one of the female students collapsed on the floor in a faint. After she had been lifted on to a bed and had revived, the consultant said to her, rather impertinently, 'What's up with you? Are you pregnant?' Whereupon two male students promptly fainted.

A consultant was asked to provide a reference about a former house physician. He wrote: 'If you get Dr Smith to work for you, you will be lucky.'

A consultant who prided himself on being able to make a spot diagnosis on the basis of a single feature in a case history was conducting a teaching out-patient clinic. He did not divulge to the audience the contents of the referral letter from the general practitioner, which read: 'Dear Dr Jones, I expect you would like to see this typical case of tabes dorsalis for teaching purposes.' He asked the nurse to bring in the next patient. Steps were heard coming down the corridor to the consulting room.

'Ah, the typical unsteady gait of tabes dorsalis, if I am not mistaken,' said the consultant to his pupils. One of the other features of this disease,' he continued glibly, 'is loss of pain in various places, such as on the nose.' At that moment a man came through the door; the consultant got up and stabbed him on the nose with a large neurological pin. The man let out a sharp yell of pain—he was the general practitioner who had come along with the patient!

A physician was examining a young girl's chest. He applied a stethoscope to her chest wall and said, 'Big breaths!'

'Yeth, and I'm only thixteen too,' lisped the girl.

"Congratulations, Dr Benson! no diagnosis, but your barium meal cholecystogram, angiogram, cardiogram, and bronchogram have rendered this patient totally radio-opaque."

Action Research for the Crippled Child is part of The National Fund for Research into Crippling Diseases

How much of a problem is crippling today?
It is estimated that a malformed child is born or a child is disabled by disease or accident every five minutes in the United Kingdom; two in every hundred infants are born disabled. This gives some idea of the size of the problem for children alone. These children very often carry their burden into adult life. Many more adults become disabled through the course of life and there are few people who will not be affected by some physical disability in their old age.

What is our purpose?
'Action Research' is a charity which raises money for medical research leading to the prevention of disability and alleviation of existing physical handicap.

What are the 'crippling diseases' referred to in the Fund's title?
Some of the better-known crippling diseases are polio, rheumatism, arthritis, Parkinson's disease, multiple sclerosis, scoliosis, spina bifida and spasticity, but there are hundreds of diseases that are known to disable. Many of these are concerned with the central nervous system,

139

but disease of the muscles, the bones and joints, the heart, the brain—indeed almost any part of the body—can be crippling.

Action Research's responsibility extends to basic and clinical research into genetic and early developmental aspects associated with, for example, muscular dystrophy or spina bifida.

Is the Fund concerned only with the prevention of crippling?
'Action Research' promotes research into the cause, prevention, cure and treatment of crippling. It can, and does, finance research into the rehabilitation of physically disabled people and also their social and environmental problems—any research project, in fact, which offers a prospect of preventing disability, a reduction of the disabling consequences of disease and injury, or improvement in the quality of life for those with an existing physical handicap.

To whom does the Fund give research grants?
Grants are usually awarded to University Departments, Hospitals and Research Institutes in the United Kingdom, but any research worker can apply to the Fund for financial support.

What are the research grants used for?
They are primarily used for salaries of research workers, research equipment and consumables. Capital grants are also awarded for the construction of new laboratories, endowment of research chairs and fellowships. Five per cent of funds are applied to the training of young scientists (not students) in research techniques.

Who approves the grants?
All applications are considered by eminent scientists— the Fund's Advisory Panels and 'College of Referees'. If the applications are recommended, their financial implications are then reviewed by the Council of the Fund who make the final decision.

Does the Fund duplicate the work of other organizations?
Care is taken that the research supported by the Fund should not duplicate but be complementary to other research. Liaison and cooperation is achieved by the Fund having observers from the Medical Research Council and Department of Health and Social Security on its scientific advisory panels and by membership of the Association of Medical Research Charities.

How much is awarded in research grants?
Over £1,500,000 during 1983 and since 1952 over £14½ million has been disbursed to research, equivalent to about £42 million at the current value of the pound.

Where does this money come from
'Action Research' is entirely dependent upon voluntary contributions. Under the banner of 'Action Research for the Crippled Child', principal support is afforded by some 1000 voluntary fund-raising committees throughout the United Kingdom. A further major contribution comes through the Cancer & Polio Research Fund from their national charity football pool, and SPARKS—Sportsmen Pledged to Aid Research into Crippling raises a substantial sum every year. Individual members of the public also make direct donations and bequests.

Investment income from money committed to future research offsets most of the Fund's administrative and fund-raising overheads and enables at least 95p in every £1 contributed to remain directly available for research.

Why is more money needed?
So much remains to be done and in the past three years calls upon 'Action Research' have more than doubled. This is a reflection of national financial stringency and the fact that there are very few voluntary organizations able to fund research after they have met their welfare commitments. Medical research has made an important contribution to reducing the incidence and burden of many severely disabling but non-fatal diseases and injuries; it must continue.

Recent Research Grants

Joint Replacement. Department of Biomedical Engineering, Institute of Orthopaedics, Royal National Orthopaedic Hospital, Stanmore £40,265

Spina Bifida. Department of Paediatrics and Child Health, University of Leeds £33,111

Genetic Disorders. Duncan Guthrie Institute of Medical Genetics, University of Glasgow £80,280

Breathing Patterns in Newborn Babies. Department of Physiology, University of Bristol £37,972

Stroke. Southampton General Hospital £21,646

Muscle Disease. Department of Physiology, University of Birmingham £37,501

Brain Damage. Department of Neurology, Royal Infirmary, Manchester £30,242

Hunter's Disease. Department of Medical Genetics, University Hospital of Wales £22,797

Congenital Dislocation of the Hip. Musgrave Park Hospital, Belfast £25,000.

These are just a few of over 200 research projects currently supported by 'Action Research'.

If you would like to help, this is the address to write to:
The National Fund for Research into Crippling Diseases,
Vincent House,
Springfield Road,
Horsham,
West Sussex, RH12 2PN